Contents

Dogs

Dogs are mammals.

Young dogs are
called puppies.

Animal Offspring

Dogs and Their Puppies

Revised Edition

Linda Tagliaferro

Raintree is an imprint of Capstone Global Library Limited, a company incorporated in England and Wales having its registered office at 264 Banbury Road, Oxford, OX2 7DY – Registered company number: 6695582

www.raintree.co.uk
myorders@raintree.co.uk

ISBN 978 1 4747 5626 6 (hardback)
22 21 20 19 18
10 9 8 7 6 5 4 3 2 1

ISBN 978 1 4747 5636 5 (paperback)
23 22 21 20 19
10 9 8 7 6 5 4 3 2 1

British Library Cataloging in Publication Data
A full catalogue record for this book is available from the British Library.

Editorial Credits
Gina Kammer, editor; Sarah Bennett, designer; Morgan Walters, media researcher; Katy LaVigne, production specialist

Printed and bound in India

Acknowledgements
We would like to thank the following for permission to reproduce photographs:
Shutterstock: Anna Goroshnikova, right 21, Anna Hoychuk, 15, Burry van den Brink, 19 , Christian Mueller, Cover, Fernando Castelani, right 20, left 21, framsook, 5, Grigorita Ko, 1, 17, Kristin Castenschiold, 7, Nadya Chetah, 9, Nixx Photography, left 20, Sarune Kairyte, 11, Stephen Coburn, 13

Every effort has been made to contact copyright holders of material reproduced in this book. Any omissions will be rectified in subsequent printings if notice is given to the publisher.

Male and female dogs mate.
Female dogs give birth
to a litter of puppies.

Puppies

Puppies cannot see
or hear until they are
about ten days old.

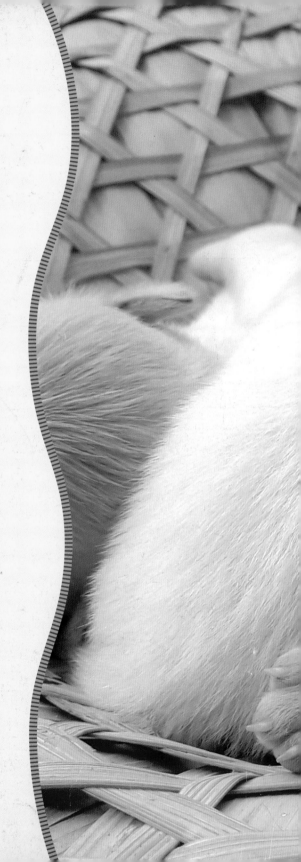

Puppies sleep most of the time. Puppies get tired from playing.

Puppies drink milk
from their mother
for about five weeks.

Growing up

Puppies can eat dog food when they are about six weeks old.

Puppies jump on and play with each other. They chew toys.

Puppies become adults
after one to two years.

Watch dogs grow

birth

adult after about two years

Glossary

adult animal that is able to mate

litter group of puppies born at the same time to the same mother; dogs usually have litters of four to six puppies

mammal warm-blooded animal that has a backbone; most mammals have hair or fur; female mammals feed milk to their young

mate join together to produce young

Find out more

Books

A Dog's Day, Rebecca Rissman (Raintree, 2014)

A Dog's Life (Watch It Grow), Louise Spilsbury (Raintree, 2011)

Dogs and Puppies (Animals and Their Babies), Annabelle Lynch (Franklin Watts, 2016)

Websites

www.animalark.co.uk/indexbafc.html?PageId=dogs
Animal Ark

www.bbc.co.uk/cbeebies/puzzles/puppy-quiz
BBC

Comprehension questions

1. What are puppies like just after they are born?

2. What is the word used for a group of puppies born at the same time?

3. How do puppies change as they grow into dogs?

Index